Italian for Opera Lovers

Sasha Newborn, editor

BANDANNA BOOKS   **2011**   **SANTA BARBARA**

BANDANNA BOOKS COLLEGE TITLES

SAPPHO: THE POEMS.* Greece's greatest lyric poet. $9.95

AREOPAGITICA: FREEDOM OF THE PRESS.* John Milton. Censorship ancient and modern. $9.95

THE APOLOGY OF SOCRATES, & THE CRITO.* Plato. $9.95

THE FIRST DETECTIVE: THREE STORIES. EDGAR ALLAN POE. Poe's amateur detective Dupin was the model for Sherlock Holmes. $12.95

DON'T PANIC: THE PROCRASTINATOR'S GUIDE TO WRITING AN EFFECTIVE TERM PAPER. Steven Posusta. $11.95

MITOS Y LEYENDAS DE MÉXICO/MYTHS AND LEGENDS OF MEXICO. Luis Leal. Twenty origin stories and history. Color plates by Álvaro Ángel Suman. $39.50

GHAZALS OF GHALIB. Ghalib's witty couplets, arguing with God, his beloved. $9.95

THE MERCHANT OF VENICE. William Shakespeare. Modernized by Rachel Burke. $11.95

GANDHI ON THE GITA. M.K. Gandhi explains the Bhagavad Gita chapter by chapter. $9.95

LEAVES OF GRASS, 1855 edition.* Walt Whitman. $11.95

ITALIAN FOR OPERA LOVERS. Italian opera terms. $5.95

DANTE & HIS CIRCLE. D. G. Rossetti. Italian love sonnets & Dante's Vita Nuova. $12.95

Order through our website at **www.bandannabooks.com/bbooks**
College Bookstores: fax orders for 5 or more copies to 805-899-2145

*Teacher supplements available.

FOREWORD

A word of warning: You will not learn to speak Italian from this book, but you can enrich your understanding of the mysteries of opera. Originally intended to be a revival of ancient Greek theater by a small group of sixteenth-century enthusiasts, opera became an art form in its own right, heavily influenced by the Baroque period in which it was born. Today the opera industry flourishes mightily in centers around the world.

But although an opera buff may know an entire opera by heart, many details of technique or intention remain hidden. This wordbook is meant to enhance one's knowledge —it is a simple compilation of Italian terms used to describe opera, and I owe a debt to prior work done by Harold Rosenthal, John Warrack, C.O. Sylvester Mawson, Ethan Mordden, and other lovers of opera.

Sasha Newborn
August 1994 /August 2011

PRONUNCIATION

Italian pronunciation is reasonably straightforward. A few accents on words spelled the same indicate that they are pronounced differently (e = and, é = is). Every letter except h is sounded, an important factor in singing.

The typical Italian syllable is consonant-vowel (Ro-ma, Mi-la-no); nearly every word ends with a vowel. An Italian speaks or sings with greater tension in the mouth than Americans are used to, always returning to a neutral position ready for a vowel. Italian vowels don't waver or slur, and are never rounded (rah-o-oo-ndi-ud), as in American English (A-i-eeng-gli-ee-ush).

THE VOWELS

a as in f*a*ther   BUT NEVER as in bat or fate
e as in l*e*t   BUT NEVER silent as in cape,
è (open) as in l*e*t   AND NEVER as in heed or the
é (close) as in h*ey*
i as in mach*i*ne   BUT NEVER as in bit or bite
i (unstressed before vowel) as *y* in yard, NOT as in ion
o as in s*o*ft   BUT NEVER as in of or hood
ò (open) as in s*o*ft
ó (close) as in r*o*pe
u as in r*u*le   BUT NEVER as in uh-huh
u (unstressed before vowel) as *w* in wall

THE CONSONANTS

Consonants are sounded forward in the mouth. Double consonants are given nearly double the amount of time (*not-te*).

NOT A PROBLEM, NO DIFFERENCE
    b sounds as baby   *n* as in nine
    d as in did   *p* as in papa

f as in food   *t* as in tight
k as in kick   *v* as in verve
m as in mama   *x* as in box (occurs rarely)
qu as in quick

SLIGHT DIFFERENCE
h is always silent, as in honest
l (with tongue behind upper front teeth)
w (occurs rarely) is pronounced as *v*
z sounds like *ts* as in Nazi or bets,
        or like *dz* (voiced) as in adze

BIG DIFFERENCE
r is just a quick flap with the tip of the tongue on the gum
ridge behind the front upper teeth. IT IS NEVER r as in red
or bird or butter.

c (before e or i) sounds like *ch* as in chair
        otherwise c sounds like *k* as in kick
ch sounds like *k* as in kick
cc sounds like *tch* as in atchoo!
g (before e or i) sounds like *j* as in jam
        otherwise *g* sounds like *g* in gag
gh sounds like *g* in gag
gli sounds like *lli* in million
gn sounds like *ni* in opinion
gg (before e or i) sounds like *dj* as in adjust
s (initial before vowel, doubled, or followed by c, f, p, q)
        sounds like *s* as in sass
s (before b, d, g, l, m, n, r, v) sounds as *z* in is
s (between vowels, in northern Italy) as *z* in is
        (in southern Italy) as *s* in sis
        (in central Italy) as *s* or *z*
sc (before e or i) sounds like *sh* as in shoe
        otherwise *sc* sounds like *sk* as in ski
sch sounds like *sk* as in ski

A

a battuta (by the beat): in strict time

abbellimento: ornament, embellishment

abbonati (also German Abonnenten, French abonnés): subscribers to a series of operas

a beneplacito: by the performer's choice

a cappella: singing in church music style, i.e., unaccompanied

acciaccatura: grace note one-half step down from melody note

accompagnamento: accompaniment

accompagnato (accompanied): fully written accompaniment for a song

accompagnatore (m.)/**accompagnatrice** (f.): accompanist

accordo: chord

a cembalo: for the keyboard

a due voci: for two voices

affabile: in a pleasing manner

affanato: sorrowfully

affetivo: pathetic

affeto: passion, affection

affetuoso: with feeling, with warmth

affrettando: quickening the tempo

agevole: with ease

agitato: agitatedly

al fresco: in the open air

al fresco opera: outdoor opera performances

alla breve (by the breve): in quick common time

alla caccia: simulating a chase

alla capella: unaccompanied singing

all'aperto opera: outdoor opera performances

alla scozzese: in the Scottish style

alla ventura: at random

allegretto: moderately brisk

allegro: lively, brisk

allegro di molto: very quick

allegro furioso: furiously quick

allegro non tanto: lively but not too quick

allentando: slowing the tempo

allestimento: production of an opera

all' ottava (also **all' ott.**): to be sung one octave higher than written

al piacere: at leisure

al più: at the most

al segno: to the sign

al solito: as usual

al tedesco: in the German style

alto: voice, usually female, with a range from F below middle C to A below high C

a mezzo voce: at half volume, subdued

amoroso: in a tender manner

ancora (encore): again, yet

ancora una volta: once again, over again

andante: moderately slow

andantino: quicker than andante (originally, andantino meant slower than andante)

antefatto: plot exposition

a piacere: ad lib, at one's pleasure

a poco a poco: little by little

appassionato: passionately

appoggiato (propped): grace notes attached to other notes; notes connected by **portamento**

appoggiatura: grace note, embellishing note

ardente: ardent, vigorous

argomento: written summary of actions prior to the beginning of an opera; prologue

aria: solo or duet song accompanied by orchestra

aria agitata: agitated song

aria cantabile: gentle and sad song

aria declamata: statement song

aria de lamento: song of lamentation

aria del sonno: song sung to sleeping one

aria del sorbetto: song during which one may go to the refreshment stand for a sorbet or ice

aria di carattere: expressive song

aria di catalogo: song consisting mainly of a list

aria di imitazione: imitating song

aria di mezzo carattere: moderately expressive song

aria di sentimento: sentimental song

aria di sortita: exit song

aria infuriata: song of anger

aria parlante (Sprechsang): speaking song; declamatory song

aria senza accompanamento: song with no accompaniment

arietta: song for a humble character; short air

ariette: short easy aria

ariette da camera: song to be sung at home

arioso: gaily, melodiously; sung speech

Arlecchino (Harlequin): leading character or "mask" in Commedia dell'Arte

assai: enough, very

a tempo: in time

a tempo giusto: in strict time

attorno attorno: here, there and everywhere

avere dei bei filati: to be skillful at holding a tone evenly

azione sacra: religious opera

azione teatrale: festival play

B

bagnio: whorehouse

barcarolle (boat song): originally from Venetian gondoliers, a 6/8 song with strong and weak beats

baritono: baritone, middle range male singing voice, from C to A-flat

basso buffo: male voice, range F to F

basso cantante: deep male voice, range F to F

basso comico: male voice, range F to F

basso profundo: male voice with range D to E

bel canto (beautiful singing): heartfelt song emphasizing full tone, smooth phrasing; traditional Italian style

beneficenza: benefit to help out an organization or individual

beneficiata: performance to allow one performer to display his/her talents in various pieces

ben marcato: well marked; marked for emphasis

bis (from Latin, twice, again): the cry for encore in Europe

bocca chiusa (closed mouth): humming. Usually a practice technique, but occasionally used in operas

bravura: spirit, bravery; florid music requiring technical virtuosity

brillante: sparkling, brilliant

brindisi (from **far brindisi**, to drink to one's health): drinking song

brio: vivacity, animation

buca: prompter's box, usually in the middle of the footlights, shielded from the audience

buffa: female singer of comic roles; opera buffa, comic opera

buffo/buffi (buffoon, from Latin **bufo**: toad, the skin of which was used to make inflated gloves for theatrical beating): male singer of comic roles, usually a fat singer

buffone: comic actor

burla (joke): comic intermezzo

burletta: burlesque operetta; comic intermezzo

burlettina: comic intermezzo

C

cabaletta: short, simple aria, or the quick last section of an aria; often follows **cavatina** and **recitative**

caccia: a chase

cadenza: intricate embellishment in an aria, originally of the singer's own invention. At a later date, composers wrote out **cadenzas.**

cadenza d'inganno: cadence on an unexpected scale; deceptive cadence

calando: becoming softer and slower

calmato: quiet, calm

caloroso: with warmth

camerata (society): the original group around Giovanni de' Bardi and Jacopo Corsi that gave rise to the idea of opera, by a revival of the spirit of Greek drama.

cantabile: flowingly

cantatore: male professional singer

cantatrice: female professional singer

cantilena (lullaby): songlike passage in a choral piece, or a solo song

canto: song; the vocal line carrying melody or expression

canto figurato: vocal ornamentation of the music, often by runs or trills

canzona overtura: Venetian opera opener, with slow and fast movements

canzone, canzoni (Provençal **canzo**): a song in its own right; ballad, lyric

canzonetta: simple song

Capitano Spavento (Captain Horrible): character in the classic Commedia dell'Arte

capo: head, beginning

capriccio: caprice

capriccioso: in a free, fantastic style

carità: feeling, tenderness

carnival (from Latin **carnem levare**: putting meat away): period of festivities before Lent

cartellone (large poster or placard): the season's list of operas to be performed

castrato, also **evirato** (castrated): a male singer castrated before the male voice change of puberty. This operation results in a singer with powerful soprano or contralto range. This practice died out by the early nineteenth century. No modern voice can adequately match the castrato voice in the music written for the castrati.

cavaletta: short aria. See **cabaletta**

cavalier servente (serving gentleman): lover of a married woman

cavata (extraction): a short expressive passage at the end of a long recitative

cavatina: simple sentimental aria; song-like air; the first slow section of an aria scene

cembalo, cembali: harpsichord, pianoforte

cercar la nota (to look for the note): anticipatory grace notes

cereni (**cero**: candle): cheap libretti sold at the stage door

chiamata: curtain call, singers bow to audience applause

chiarezza: clearness, brightness

chiedere un bis: to call for an encore performance

chorus (from the Greek Χορος): dance or dancers

coda: concluding section of music

codetta: a short coda

col canto: with the melody or vocal part

colla destra: with the right hand

colla parte (with the part): instruction for accompanists to follow the lead of the singer for tempo

coll' arco: with the bow

colla sinistra: with the left hand

colla voce (with the voice): instruction to accompanists to follow the singer's tempo and expressive touches

collegno (with the wood): playing a stringed instrument with the wooden stock of the bow, rather than with the gut strings

Colombina: character in Commedia dell'Arte

coloratura (from German **Koloratur**): vocal elaboration by quick light runs or trills. Also known as **canto figurato** or **fioritura**

come prima: as at first

come sopra: as above

Commedia dell'Arte: 16th century Italian stage performances of improvised comedy with archetypal characters or "masks." Typical characters include Arlecchio (Harlequin, a little fool), Pantalone the magnifico (a Venetian merchant), Brighella (a cunning Bergamese), Scapino (cowardly), Scaramuccia (from Naples), Pulcinella (also from Naples), Capitano Spavento (Captain Horrible), Gratiano the doctor (gullible pedant), Colombina the servant, and the hero Fulvio or Fortunio. Common plots were mistaken identities, disguises, twins, lovers who turn out to be brother and sister. Many elements of Commedia dell'Arte also appear in opera.

commedia per musica (comedy for music): comic opera (18th century term)

commodo: quietly

comprimario (with the main one): secondary role, or any small part

con amore: tenderly

con brio: with vivacity

con calore: passionately, with warmth

concertante: a concerto in which two or more voices or solo instruments alternately take the principal part

concertino: a small concerto

concerto: a composition written for one or more principal instruments

con dolcezza: with sweetness

con dolore: with grief, sadly

con expressione: expressively

con forza: with vigor

congiura (conspiracy): scene of plotting or conspiring

con grazia: gracefully

con gusto: tastefully

con impeto: impetuously

con molto passione: with much passion

con moto: energetically, with animation

con prestezza: rapidly

con semplicità: with simplicity

con sordino: with a mute (on a violin), or soft-pedaled (on a keyboard)

con spirito: spiritedly, with animation

continuato: continued, sustained

continuo: basso continuo. The bass part played by harpsichord or cello to accompany **recitative**

contrabasso: double bass

contralto (against the alto): lowest female voice range

contratenor: countertenor; high male voice range, using head resonance; similar in range to the contralto and soprano ranges

corda/corde: string

corno: horn

corno di bassetto: basset horn

corno inglese: English horn

corona: a held note or chord

crescendo (growing; also written as **cr., cresc.**): gradually increasing loudness

D

da capo (also written as **D.C.**): from the beginning

da capo al fine: from beginning to the end

da capo al segno: from the beginning to the sign

da capo aria: first song of an opera

da cappelo: in church style

da chiesa: in church style

dal segno (from the sign): repeat from the sign

damigella (damsel): pretty but impertinent maid role; related to the **soubrette**

decrescendo (also **dec., decres.**): gradual decrease of loudness

desto: lively, sprightly

deus ex machina (Latin: the god out of the machine): theatrical device of lowering a god from above to resolve a dilemma; also, any last-minute solution to a tangled plot

di bravura: with brilliance, floridly

di grado in grado: step by step, gradually

diluendo: dying away

diminuendo: gradually diminishing volume

di molto: very

direttore d'orchestra: conductor

di salto: at a leap

disinvolto: free, graceful, spirited

diva (goddess): prima donna

divertimento: entertainment, diversion

divisi: divided, separate; music written differently for several performers

dolcemente: sweetly, softly

dolce-piccante: bittersweet

dolente: sad, plaintive

doloroso: pathetic, dolorous

dopo: after

doppio: double, twofold

doppio movimento: twice as fast as preceding movement

dotazione (endowment): all-purpose sets used in more than one production

drama per musica: libretto for a serious musical opera (18th century term)

dramma glocoso: comic opera with serious parts (18th century term)

due volte: turn twice

duet: song for two singers

duetto da camera: song for two voices sung at home; opera later incorporated this song form.

duodrama: play for two actors, with musical accompaniment

duramente: harshly

E

elenco artistico (catalog of artists): the list of performers, technicians, and others in a company, or those in a particular production or season.

energicamente (also **energ.**): with energy

energico: energetic, forceful

enfaticamente: emphatically

ente autonomo (autonomous being): opera house business management

equabilmente: smoothly, equably

eroico, eroica: heroic

erotico, erotica: love song

espressione: expression

espressivo: expressive, with expression

evirato (unmanned, castrated). Male singer castrated before puberty. See **castrato**

F

falcon (from Marie-Cornélie Falcon): sturdy female range from top of soprano to lower mezzo-soprano.

falsetto (from Italian **falso**: altered, false, Latin **fauces**: throat): high male voice range induced by limiting the vocal cords

falsettone: falsetto singer

falsetto rinforzato: falsetto singer

fantoccino, fantoccini: puppet, marionette; simpleton

fastoso: pompous, stately

favola in musica: opera based on myth or legend (17th century term)

favola per musica: opera based on myth

fermata (stop, pause): a note or chord sung or played longer than usual

festivamente: gaily

fiato: breath

filar il tuono (spin the tone): to hold a tone evenly

filar la voce (spin the voice): to hold the voice on a tone, neither increasing nor decreasing volume

finale (end): the last movement in an operatic act, usually climactic, incorporating elements that preceded it, and often dramatically overstated

fine (also **fin.**): the end, finish

fioco: faint, hoarse

fioreggiante: floridly

fiorito: flowery, florid

fioritura, fioriture (flourishes): vocal ornamentation of the written score, sometimes written; coloratura

flebile: plaintive, mournful

flebilmente: mournfully

focosamente: in a fiery manner, vehemently

focoso: passionate, fiery

forte: loud

forte forte: very loud
forte-piano: loud and then soft
forte possibile: as loud as possible
fortissimo (also **ff.**): very loud
forza: power, vigor
forzando. See **sforzando**
freddamente: coldly
fregiatura: embellishment
frescamente: freshly, vigorously
frottola: ballad
fuoco: fire, passion
furiosamente: passionately, vehemently

G

gajamente: gayly
galantemente: gallantly, gracefully
gaudioso: joyful
gentile: graceful, delicate
giochevole: playful, merry
giocondo: playful, gay
giocoso: lively, mirthful
giovale: jovial, gay
glissando: gliding up and down the scale
grosso: full, great, grand
gruppetto: rapid singing of a note alternated with the notes
    immediately above and below it
gustosamente: tastefully

I

imbroglio (intrigue, entanglement, from the Broglio, part of the Doge of Venice's palace): chaotic scene with contrasting melodies or rhythms

impazientemente: impatiently

imperioso: imperious, haughty

impetuoso: impetuous, dashing

impresario (from impresa: enterprise): manager of opera company; organizer

improvvisata: impromptu composition, improvisation

in alt: the octave above the top of the treble staff, G to F

in altissimo: the octave above the **in alt** octave, G to F

indiscrezioni: prospectus of the coming season

intermedio, intermedi: one-act comic play between acts of an opera

intermezzo (interlude): short independent music piece in the middle of a drama or opera seria; this contrasting comic drama led to opera buffa. Also, an interlude or digression of music or drama inserted between scenes

Italian overture: allegro, adagio, allegro movements, known as **sinfonia**; originated by Alessandro Scarlatti

L

la commedia è finita (the comedy is ended): last words of *I Pagliacci*

lagrimoso: tearfully, plaintively

l'allegro: the cheerful man

lamentando: lamenting, sorrowful

lamentevole: plaintive, doleful

lamento (lament): tragic aria usually before the climax and dénouement

lamentoso: sorrowful, mournful

languente: languishing, faint

languidamente: languidly, faintly

largamente: broadly

larghetto: somewhat slowly; tempo between **adagio** and **largo**

larghissimo: very slowly

largo (broad): solemn, slow; stately movement

lazzo, lazzi (joke): improvised solo acting, especially in the Commedia dell'Arte; comic opera librettists incorporated some of these routines into their operas

legatissimo: very smoothly

legato (connected): smoothly, flowing style of singing, with no breaks between notes

leggiero: light, nimble, delicate

lentamente: slowly

lentando: becoming slower, retarding

lento: slow, slowly

liberamente: freely, liberally

libretto (little book): the book of the spoken and sung words of an opera. Copies are sometimes made for sale at performances. Most libretti are not original stories, but take their plots from plays, novels, narrative poems, or actual incidents.

licenza (permission): license, freedom of style; a 17th century tradition of appending a final chorus in praise of the patron or dedicatee of the opera

lieto fine (happy ending): last-minute, usually improbable, turn of the plot toward a happy resolution, often by means of a deus ex machina

lusigando, lusigante: alluring, soothing, caressing

luttuosamente: mournfully, sadly

luttuoso: mournful, doleful

M

madrigal opera: series of madrigals strung together by a loose plot; a primitive form of opera

maestosamente: with dignity, majestically

maestoso (also **maes.**): majestic, grandiose

maestro (master): title of respect for composer, teacher, conductor, or impresario

maestro al cembalo: master at the keyboard, usually harpsichord

maestro collaboratore: musical assistant

maestro concertatore: conductor

maestro di cappella (master of the chapel): **Kappelmeister**; church music director

maestro di coro: choirmaster

maestro sostituto: coach or musical assistant

maestro suggeritore: prompter who gives cues to singers on every phrase; he/she also repeats the conductor's rhythm

mancando (also **man., manc.**): failing, languishing, dying away

marcato: marked, accented, distinct

martellato (hammered): strongly marked

marziale (martial): in warlike style

masque: court entertainment using music, dance, acting, singing in mythological settings, with scenery; a popular form in the 16th and 17th centuries

mattinata: morning song; **aubade**

melodramma: opera of 17th century; also, 19th century Romantic revival of **opera seria,** but de-emphasizing arias in favor of plot movement

meno, men: less

meno mosso: less quick

messa di voce (placing of voice): gradual crescendo or

diminuendo on a single sustained note, one of the marks of bel canto

metaphor aria: aria elaborating on a metaphor or simile

mezza voce (half voice): sung in a muted fashion

mezzo: middle, half, medium

mezzo forte (also **mf.**): moderately loud

mezzo piano (also **mp.**): moderately soft

mezzo-soprano (medium soprano): middle female voice range

mezzo voce (also **m.v.**): with medium volume

minaccevolmente: menacingly

minacciando: threateningly

misterioso: mysterious

misurato: measured, in strict time

mollemente: softly, gently

molto: much, very

molto allegro: very quick

morbidezza (pathos): sentimental opera; similar to verismo, but not violent

morendo: dying away

mormorando: murmuring, whispering

mosso: with motion, rapid, quicker

moto: energy, motion

N

Neapolitan opera: a school of 18th century composers centered around Naples, who used **recitative** and **da capo** arias and a few duets but rarely used ensemble singing. Texts by Metastasio, for instance, teem with stock characters. Naples also was known for lively **opera buffa.**

nota: note

nota buona: accented note

nota cattiva: unaccented note

nota sensibile: leading note

nota sostenuta: sustained note

notturno: nocturne

number opera: an opera in which spoken dialogue is interrupted by separate musical numbers. By the beginning of the 19th century, music was integrated into dramatic action throughout an opera.

nuovo allestimento: a new production of an older work

O

obbligato (indispensable, bound): an instrumental part that cannot be left out, even though it is simply an accompaniment to the singer.

ombra scene: scene with a ghost (**ombra**), or in Hell

opera (work): a costume drama usually sung to instrumental accompaniment

opera buffa (comic opera): opera with comic plot of ordinary characters (i.e., not nobility or gods). **Opera buffa** had its origins in short comic scenes or **intermezzi** in **opera seria,** but developed into an independent genre.

opera in musica (**opera**, for short): a sung drama with instrumental accompaniment

opera semiseria: opera with comic as well as serious aspects

opera seria: Classical serious opera, the main form of opera in the 17th and 18th centuries. Historical drama, pageantry, nobility and gods prevailed. **Arias** and **recitatives** carry most of the action.

operetta (little opera): comic opera or play with overture, dance, songs and interludes

orchestra (Greek ᾿ορχηστρα): area in front of the stage from which the chorus commented on the action. The usual opera chorus has soprano, contralto, tenor and bass sections.

orchestra pit: area in front of and below the stage, for the orchestra to sit

ornamentation: embellishment of melody line, improvised by customary rules. By the 18th century, ornamentation had become extreme, and composers began to write more exactly what they intended should be sung.

ornamenti: ornaments, embellishments, grace notes

ornatamente: with embellishments, floridly

overtura (opening): Instrumental opening for an opera. Originally the overtura simply consisted of flourishes. By the 18th century, composers began to incorporate elements of the music to come in the overture.

P

padre nobile (noble father): formerly, the role representing a figure of authority

padrone: master, captain

palchettone: large box used for general purposes

palco (platform): theater boxes on the sides of theater walls, reserved for special members of the audience

palco della vedova (widow's box): theater box concealing its occupants from the rest of the audience

palco di pepiano: box on stage level

palco di proscenio: stage box

palco reale (also **palco ducale, palco governativo, palco eletorale**): royal theater box

pantomime (Greek παντομιμος): drama with no speech; dumb show

parlando (speaking): **Sprechsang**, song in speaking style

parlato (spoken): spoken dialogue in an opera

parody: caricature, comic version of a serious piece. In the 18th century, parody productions were often staged simultaneously with the objects of their satire

passacaglia: variations sung over a repetitive pattern

pasticcio (pie): pastiche; musical play with numbers by or adapted from several composers; popular in the 18th century.

pastorale: play on mythic or rural subject; later pastorales were written with music and dance

pertichino (understudy): silent or listening character during **recitative**; now obsolete

pesante: heavily, gravely

pezzo, pezzi (pl.): musical piece, excerpt

piacevole: pleasing

piangendo: weepingly, plaintively

pianissimo: very softly

piano: softly; keyboard instrument (originally pianoforte)

piffero, pifferi: fife; organ stop simulating a fife

più: more

più allegro: quicker

più lento: slower

più mosso: quicker, with more animation

pizzicato: plucked by the fingers rather than bowed

poco (little): somewhat

poco allegro: somewhat quick

poco a poco: little by little

poco forte: somewhat loud

poco più lento: somewhat slower

ponticello (little bridge): in **bel canto**, the shift in range between chest and head registers; also, the bridge of a stringed instrument

portamento: smooth glide of voice from one note to another

portato (carried): sustained

preciso: with precision

prelude (Latin: **praeludium**): overture, piece that goes before

presa (taking): a mark showing where successive voices join the singing

prestissimo: very quickly

presto: quickly, faster than allegro

prima buffa: leading female comic singer

prima donna (first lady): female lead in an opera, or principal soprano of an opera company

prima volta: first time

primo uomo, prim'omo: leading male singer

protesta (protest, statement): a statement printed in librettos during the 17th and 18th centuries stating that the author was a true Roman Catholic despite poetic license with pagan deities

prova (trial): rehearsal of a production

prova generale: dress rehearsal to which critics and the public are admitted

puppet opera: opera performed by puppets

Q

quodlibet (Latin, that which pleases): musical game of spontaneously putting together various melodies; popular until the 18th century

R

raddolcendo (also **raddol.**): becoming softer

rallentando (also **ral., rall., rallo.**): gradually slower

rammentatore: prompter

rappresentazione: acted oratorio, one of the preceding forms of opera

rataplan: sound of a drum

recitando: declamatory, recitation

recitativo: the basic declamatory singing style of early opera and oratorio; heightened speech. **Recitativo** may range from almost fully speaking to fully accompanied singing (**recitativo stromentato**)

recitativo accompagnato (accompanied song): song with fully orchestrated accompaniment

recitativo arioso: melodious speech

recitativo secco (dry song): sung dialogue with simple chordal accompaniment by a single harpsichord or cello

recitativo stromentato: sung dialogue with musical accompaniment

reminiscence motive: short theme of a person repeated later in the production

replicato: repeated, doubled

rinforzando (reinforcing; also written as **rf., rfz., rinf.**): giving additional stress

ripieno (filling up): supplementary, additional

ripostamente: restfully, calmly

risvegliato: awakened, with renewed animation

ritardando (also **rit., ritard.**): becoming slower

ritenuto (also **rit., riten.**): held back, gradually slowing

ritornello (little return): brief instrumental prelude or refrain to an aria performed by instruments only

romanza (romance): love aria or soliloquy, rarely embellished

rondo (round): song with recurring theme

rondoletto: short rondo

rubato (robbed): technique of pushing or slowing the tempo to show expression

S

sacra rappresentazione: acted oratorio

saltarello: lively hopping dance

scena (Greek σκηνη: stage): opera scene; dramatic **recitative** interspersed with melodic passages; solo less formal than an aria to advance the plot line

scenario (scenery): outline libretto profiling the characters, and showing number and type of scenes

scherzando: playfully

scherzo (pleasantry, joke): sprightly passage, usually following a slow one

scintillante: sparkling

sciolto: freely, independently

scordato: untuned; played out of tune

scordatura: tuning an instrument to an odd scale

scorrendo: gliding

scusi, scuzate, scusatemi: pardon me, excuse me

sdegnoso: scornful, disdainful

seconda volta: second time

segno (sign): sign marking beginning or end of repetition

segue: follows, now follows

sempre (also **semp.**): always, continually

senza: without

senza replica: without repetition

senza sordini: without mutes

senza stromenti: without instruments

senza tempo: without strict time

seraglio: harem

serenata (evening song): originally, song sung under a lady's window; any light instrumental piece

sforzando, sforzato (forcing/forced; also written as **sf., sfz., sforz.**): with emphasis, accented

sino: to, as far as

sino al segno: to the sign

slentando (also **slent.**): slackening in tempo

slumber scene: in 17th century, a scene with a character asleep on the stage, addressed by a ghost or spirit

smaniante: passionate, furious

smorzando, smorzato (also **smorz.**): dying away

soave, soavemente: sweetly, tenderly

soggetto, soggetti: subject, theme

solfeggio (sol-fa singing): practicing scales

soprano (**sopra**: above): highest female voice range

soprano drammatico: range G to C

soprano leggiero: range G to F

soprano lirico: range B-flat to C

soprano lirico spinto: range A to C#

sordamente: softly, in a muffled manner

sordino: a violin mute

sordo: muted, muffled

sospirando, sospirante: sighing, longing

sospiroso: sighing

sostenuto (also **sos., sost.**): sustained

sotto voce (below the voice): in an undertone, soft singing

soubrette: coquettish maid; soprano in supporting role

sovrintendente (superintendent): business manager of an Italian opera house

spianato (levelled): even, smooth

spiccato: distinctly detached, half-staccato bowing

spinto (pushed): a voice, usually tenor or soprano, pushed to its limits of volume or expressiveness

spirito: spirit, fire

spiritoso: spiritedly

sprezzatura (scornfulness): informal expressive manner of singing

squarcio di vita (slice of life): realism in opera

staccato (detached): distinctly sounded separate notes; opposite of **legato** style

stagione: season

stagione lirica: opera season; implies that the same cast will perform throughout the season, i.e., not a repertory system

stesso: the same

stile rappresentativo: term in early opera for dramatic speech set to music

stinguendo: dying away

strepitoso: noisy, loud, impetuous

stretto, stretta, stretti (squeezing): quickening of tempo at end of a movement; intense finale

stromenti: instruments

stromenti da arco: bowed string instruments

stromenti da fiato: wind instruments

stromenti da percossa: percussion instruments

stromenti da tasto: keyboard instruments
stromenti di corda: stringed instruments
stromenti di legno: wood instruments
subitamente: suddenly, at once
subito: in haste, quickly
susurrando, susurrante: whispering, murmuring
svegliato: sprightly, briskly

T

tantarella: lively whirling dance
tanto: so much, as much
tardamente: slowly, lingeringly
tardando: lingering, slowing tempo
tempo: time, musical time measured in beats per minute
tempo comodo: in moderate time
tempo de marcia: march time
tempo di ballo: in dance time
tempo di menuetto: minuet time
tempo di prima parte: at the same speed as the first part
tempo giusto: in correct time
tempo primo: first time
tempo rubato (robbed time): rhythm in which some notes
    are lengthened at the expense of others
teneramente: tenderly
tenerezza: tenderness
tenore: highest natural male range C to C
tenore buffo: comic tenor, male singing range C to B-flat
tenore di forza: male range C to C
tenore di grazia: male range C to D
tenore lirico spinto: an exceptionally powerful tenor voice
tenore robusto: powerful tenor
tenore spinto: male singing range C to C
tenuto (held; also written as ten.): sustained, to hold a note
    for its full value or a little more

terzetto: trio

tessitura (texture): the range of a musical piece compared with the voice range it was written for

timoroso: hesitant, timorous

timpani: drums

timpani coperti: muffled drums

tinta (hue): sound coloration

tosto: quick, rapid

tranquillamente: tranquilly

travesti (disguised): trouser-role; role in which a woman is dressed as a man

tre corde: release of piano's soft pedal

tremando: tremulously, in a tremolo manner

tremolando: using tremolo

tremolo: trembling or quavering

trillo caprino (goat's trill): a single note trilled, or two notes a semitone apart alternated rapidly

tristezza: sadness, melancholy

troppo: too much

turco: in Turkish style

tutta forza: with full force

tutti: all together

tutto solo: all by itself

U

umore: humor, playfulness

una corda (one string): using the soft pedal on the piano

una volta: once

V

veloce: with great rapidity

verismo (realism): turn of the century naturalistic school of opera, aiming to show **squarcio di vita**, a slice of life

vibrato (vibrated): forcible; small rapid variations in pitch produced by tension

vigoroso: with vigor

vivace: lively, spirited

vivo: with life, lively

voce: voice

voce bianca (white voice): voices of women and children

voce di petto: chest register

voce di testa: head register

voce granita: firm voice

voce mista: mixed voice

voce pastosa: soft flexible voice

voce spiccata: clearly enunciated voice

voce velata (veiled voice): obscured voice

volante (flying): with light rapidity

volata (flight): rapid series of embellishing notes

volta, volte: turning, time

volteggiando: crossing hands in playing at the keyboard

volti subito (also **v.s.**): turn over quickly

Z

zufolo: small flute

www.ingramcontent.com/pod-product-compliance
Lightning Source LLC
Chambersburg PA
CBHW030011040426
42337CB00012BA/738